UNFAIR CONTRACT TERMS ACT 1977 (UK)

Updated as of March 26, 2018

THE LAW LIBRARY

TABLE OF CONTENTS

Introductory Text	4
PART I AMENDMENT OF LAW FOR ENGLAND AND WALES AND NORTHERN IRELAND	4
Scope of Part I.	10
Interpretation of Part I.	11
PART II AMENDMENT OF LAW FOR SCOTLAND	11
Scope of Part II.	18
Interpretation of Part II.	19
PART III PROVISIONS APPLYING TO WHOLE OF UNITED KINGDOM	20
Schedules	22
Schedule 1. Scope of Sections 2 , 3 and 7	23
Schedule 2. "Guidelines" for Application of Reasonableness Test	24
Schedule 3. Amendments of Enactments	25
Schedule 4. Repeals	25
Open Government Licence v3.0	26

Introductory Text

Unfair Contract Terms Act 1977

1977 CHAPTER 50

An Act to impose further limits on the extent to which under the law of England and Wales and Northern Ireland civil liability for breach of contract, of for negligence or other breach of duty, can be avoided by means of contract terms and otherwise, and under the law of Scotland civil liability can be avoided by means of contract terms.
[26th October 1977]
Commencement Information
I1. Act not in force at Royal Assent; Act wholly in force at 1.2.1978 see s. 31. (1)

PART I AMENDMENT OF LAW FOR ENGLAND AND WALES AND NORTHERN IRELAND

PART I +N.I. AMENDMENT OF LAW FOR ENGLAND AND WALES AND NORTHERN IRELAND

Modifications etc. (not altering text)
C1. Pt. I applied (3.1.1995): by 1973 c. 13, s. 11. A (as inserted (3.1.1995) by 1994 c. 35, ss. 7, 8. (2)(3), Sch. 2 para. 4. (6)); by 1979 c. 54, s. 61. (5. A) (as inserted (3.1.1995) by 1994 c. 35, ss. 7, 8. (2)(3), Sch. 2 para. 5. (9)(c)); by 1982 c. 29, s. 18. (3) (as inserted (3.1.1995) by 1994 c. 35, ss. 7, 8. (2)(3), Sch. 2 para. 6. (10))

1 Scope of Part I.+N.I.

(1) For the purposes of this Part of this Act, "negligence" means the breach—
  (a) of any obligation, arising from the express or implied terms of a contract, to take reasonable care or exercise reasonable skill in the performance of the contract;
  (b) of any common law duty to take reasonable care or exercise reasonable skill (but not any stricter duty);
  (c) of the common duty of care imposed by the M1 Occupiers' Liability Act 1957 or the M2 Occupiers' Liability Act (Northern Ireland) 1957.
F1. (2)This Part of this Act is subject to Part III; and in relation to contracts, the operation of sections 2 [F1 , 3] and 7 is subject to the exceptions made by Schedule 1.
(3) In the case of both contract and tort, sections 2 to 7 apply (except where the contrary is stated in section 6. (4)) only to business liability, that is liability for breach of obligations or duties

arising—
> (a) from things done or to be done by a person in the course of a business (whether his own business or another's); or
>
> (b) from the occupation of premises used for business purposes of the occupier;

and references to liability are to be read accordingly [F2but liability of an occupier of premises for breach of an obligation or duty towards a person obtaining access to the premises for recreational or educational purposes, being liability for loss or damage suffered by reason of the dangerous state of the premises, is not a business liability of the occupier unless granting that person such access for the purposes concerned falls within the business purposes of the occupier].

(4) In relation to any breach of duty or obligation, it is, immaterial for any purpose of this Part of this Act whether the breach was inadvertent or intentional, or whether liability for it arises directly or vicariously.

Amendments (Textual)

F1. Words in s. 1. (2) substituted (1.10.2015 for specified purposes, 1.10.2016 in so far as not already in force) by Consumer Rights Act 2015 (c. 15), s. 100. (5), Sch. 4 para. 3; S.I. 2015/1630, arts. 3. (g), 4. (c) (with art. 6. (1)(2))

F2. Words added by Occupiers' Liability Act 1984 (c. 3, SIF 122:2), s. 2 (E.W.) and by the Occupiers' Liability (Northern Ireland) Order 1987 S.I. 1987/1280 (N.I.15), art 4

Marginal Citations

M11957 c. 31

M21957 c. 25 (N.I.)

Avoidence of liability for negligence, breach of contract, etc.+N.I.

2 Negligence liability.+N.I.

(1) A person cannot by reference to any contract term or to a notice given to persons generally or to particular persons exclude or restrict his liability for death or personal injury resulting from negligence.

(2) In the case of other loss or damage, a person cannot so exclude or restrict his liability for negligence except in so far as the term or notice satisfies the requirement of reasonableness.

(3) Where a contract term or notice purports to exclude or restrict liability for negligence a person's agreement to or awareness of it is not of itself to be taken as indicating his voluntary acceptance of any risk.

[F3. (4)This section does not apply to—
> (a) a term in a consumer contract, or
>
> (b) a notice to the extent that it is a consumer notice,

(but see the provision made about such contracts and notices in sections 62 and 65 of the Consumer Rights Act 2015).]

Amendments (Textual)

F3. S. 2. (4) inserted (1.10.2015 for specified purposes, 1.10.2016 in so far as not already in force) by Consumer Rights Act 2015 (c. 15), s. 100. (5), Sch. 4 para. 4; S.I. 2015/1630, arts. 3. (g), 4. (c) (with art. 6. (1)(2))

Modifications etc. (not altering text)

C2. S. 2. (2) excluded (11.11.1999, but subject to s. 10. (3)of the amending Act, does not apply in relation to a contract referred to in s. 10. (2)) by 1999 c. 31, ss. 7. (2), 10. (2)(3)

3 Liability arising in contract.+N.I.

F4. (1)This section applies as between contracting parties where one of them deals F4... on the other's written standard terms of business.

(2) As against that party, the other cannot by reference to any contract term—

(a) when himself in breach of contract, exclude or restrict any liability of his in respect of the breach; or

(b) claim to be entitled—

(i) to render a contractual performance substantially different from that which was reasonably expected of him, or

(ii) in respect of the whole or any part of his contractual obligation, to render no performance at all,

except in so far as (in any of the cases mentioned above in this subsection) the contract term satisfies the requirement of reasonableness.

[F5. (3)This section does not apply to a term in a consumer contract (but see the provision made about such contracts in section 62 of the Consumer Rights Act 2015).]

Amendments (Textual)

F4. Words in s. 3. (1) omitted (1.10.2015 for specified purposes, 1.10.2016 in so far as not already in force) by virtue of Consumer Rights Act 2015 (c. 15), s. 100. (5), Sch. 4 para. 5. (2); S.I. 2015/1630, arts. 3. (g), 4. (c) (with art. 6. (1)(2))

F5. S. 3. (3) inserted (1.10.2015 for specified purposes, 1.10.2016 in so far as not already in force) by Consumer Rights Act 2015 (c. 15), s. 100. (5), Sch. 4 para. 5. (3); S.I. 2015/1630, arts. 3. (g), 4. (c) (with art. 6. (1)(2))

Modifications etc. (not altering text)

C3. S. 3. (2)(b) extended (1.11.1998 and 1.7.1999 in relation to certain contracts and 7.8.2002 insofar as not then in force) by 1998 c. 20, s. 14. (2) (with s. 12); S.I. 1998/2479, arts. 2,3; S.I. 1999/1816, art. 3. (1); S.I. 2002/1673, art. 2

C4. S. 3. (2)(b) applied by 1998 c. 20, s. 58. (4) (as inserted (16.3.2013) by The Late Payment of Commercial Debts Regulations 2013 (S.I. 2013/395), regs. 1. (1), 3. (4) (with reg. 1. (3)))

F64 Unreasonable indemnity clauses.+N.I.

. . . .

Amendments (Textual)

F6. S. 4 omitted (1.10.2015 for specified purposes, 1.10.2016 in so far as not already in force) by virtue of Consumer Rights Act 2015 (c. 15), s. 100. (5), Sch. 4 para. 6; S.I. 2015/1630, arts. 3. (g), 4. (c) (with art. 6. (1)(2))

Liability arising from sale or supply of goods+N.I.

F75"Guarantee" of consumer goods.+N.I.

. . . .

Amendments (Textual)

F7. S. 5 omitted (1.10.2015) by virtue of Consumer Rights Act 2015 (c. 15), s. 100. (5), Sch. 4 para. 7; S.I. 2015/1630, art. 3. (g) (with art. 6. (1))

6 Sale and hire purchase.+N.I.

(1) Liability for breach of the obligations arising from—

(a) [F8section 12 of the Sale of Goods Act 1979](seller's implied undertakings as to title, etc.);

(b) section 8 of the M3 Supply of Goods (Implied Terms) Act 1973 (the corresponding thing in relation to hire-purchase), cannot be excluded or restricted by reference to any contract term.

[F9. (1. A)Liability for breach of the obligations arising from—

(a) section 13, 14 or 15 of the 1979 Act (seller's implied undertakings as to conformity of goods with description or sample, or as to their quality or fitness for a particular purpose);

(b) section 9, 10 or 11 of the 1973 Act (the corresponding things in relation to hire purchase),

cannot be excluded or restricted by reference to a contract term except in so far as the term satisfies the requirement of reasonableness.]

F10. (2). . . . .

F10. (3). . . . .

(4) The liabilities referred to in this section are not only the business liabilities defined by section 1. (3), but include those arising under any contract of sale of goods or hire-purchase agreement.

[F11. (5)This section does not apply to a consumer contract (but see the provision made about such contracts in section 31 of the Consumer Rights Act 2015).]

Amendments (Textual)

F8. Words substituted by Sale of Goods Act 1979 (c. 54, SIF 109:1), ss. 62, 63, Sch. 2 para. 19. (a)

F9. S. 6. (1. A) inserted (1.10.2015) by Consumer Rights Act 2015 (c. 15), s. 100. (5), Sch. 4 para. 8. (2); S.I. 2015/1630, art. 3. (g) (with art. 6. (1))

F10. S. 6. (2)(3) omitted (1.10.2015) by virtue of Consumer Rights Act 2015 (c. 15), s. 100. (5), Sch. 4 para. 8. (3); S.I. 2015/1630, art. 3. (g) (with art. 6. (1)); S.I. 2015/1630, art. 3. (g) (with art. 6. (1))

F11. S. 6. (5) inserted (1.10.2015) by Consumer Rights Act 2015 (c. 15), s. 100. (5), Sch. 4 para. 8. (4); S.I. 2015/1630, art. 3. (g) (with art. 6. (1))

Marginal Citations

M31973 c. 13.

7 Miscellaneous contracts under which goods pass.+N.I.

(1) Where the possession or ownership of goods passes under or in pursuance of a contract not governed by the law of sale of goods or hire-purchase, subsections (2) to (4) below apply as regards the effect (if any) to be given to contract terms excluding or restricting liability for breach of obligation arising by implication of law from the nature of the contract.

[F12. (1. A)Liability in respect of the goods' correspondence with description or sample, or their quality or fitness for any particular purpose, cannot be excluded or restricted by reference to such a term except in so far as the term satisfies the requirement of reasonableness.]

F13. (2). . . . .

F13. (3). . . . .

[F14. (3. A)Liability for breach of the obligations arising under section 2 of the Supply of Goods and Services Act 1982 (implied terms about title etc. in certain contracts for the transfer of the property in goods) cannot be excluded or restricted by reference to any such term.]

(4) Liability in respect of—

(a) the right to transfer ownership of the goods, or give possession; or

(b) the assurance of quiet possession to a person taking goods in pursuance of the contract,

cannot [F15. (in a case to which subsection (3. A) above does not apply)], be excluded or restricted by reference to any such term except in so far as the term satisfies the requirement of reasonableness.

[F16. (4. A)This section does not apply to a consumer contract (but see the provision made about such contracts in section 31 of the Consumer Rights Act 2015).]

(5) F17. . . . .

Amendments (Textual)

F12. S. 7. (1. A) inserted (1.10.2015) by Consumer Rights Act 2015 (c. 15), s. 100. (5), Sch. 4 para. 9. (2); S.I. 2015/1630, art. 3. (g) (with art. 6. (1))

F13. S. 7. (2)(3) omitted (1.10.2015) by virtue of Consumer Rights Act 2015 (c. 15), s. 100. (5), Sch. 4 para. 9. (3); S.I. 2015/1630, art. 3. (g) (with art. 6. (1)); S.I. 2015/1630, art. 3. (g) (with art. 6. (1))

F14. S. 7. (3. A) inserted by Supply of Goods and Services Act 1982 (c. 29, SIF 109:1), ss. 17. (2), 20. (5)

F15. Words inserted by Supply of Goods and Services Act 1982 (c. 29, SIF 109:1), ss. 17. (3), 20. (5)

F16. S. 7. (4. A) inserted (1.10.2015) by Consumer Rights Act 2015 (c. 15), s. 100. (5), Sch. 4 para. 9. (4); S.I. 2015/1630, art. 3. (g) (with art. 6. (1))

F17. S. 7. (5) repealed (E.W.) (6.4.2005) by The Regulatory Reform (Trading Stamps) Order 2005 (S.I. 2005/871), art. 6, Sch.

Other provisions about contracts+N.I.

8. X1 Misrepresentation.+N.I.

(1) In the M4 Misrepresentation Act 1967, the following is substituted for section 3—
"3 Avoidance of provision excluding liability for misrepresentation.
If a contract contains a term which would exclude or restrict—
   (a) any liability to which a party to a contract may be subject by reason of any misrepresentation made by him before the contract was made; or
   (b) any remedy available to another party to the contract by reason of sucha misrepresentation, that term shall be of no effect except in so far as it satisfies the requirement of reasonableness as stated in section 11. (1) of the Unfair Contract Terms Act 1977; and it is for those claiming that the term satisfies that requirement to show that it does.".
(2) The same section is substituted for section 3 of the M5 Misrepresentation Act (Northern Ireland) 1967.

Editorial Information
X1. The text of s. 8 is in the form in which it was originally enacted: it was not reproduced in Statutes in Force and does not reflect any amendments or repeals which may have been made prior to 1.2.1991.

Marginal Citations
M41967 c. 7
M51967 c. 14 (N.I.)

F189 Effect of breach.+N.I.

. . . .

Amendments (Textual)
F18. S. 9 omitted (1.10.2015 for specified purposes, 1.10.2016 in so far as not already in force) by virtue of Consumer Rights Act 2015 (c. 15), s. 100. (5), Sch. 4 para. 10; S.I. 2015/1630, arts. 3. (g), 4. (c) (with art. 6. (1)(2))

10 Evasion by means of secondary contract.+N.I.

A person is not bound by any contract term prejudicing or taking away rights of his which arise under, or in connection with the performance of, another contract, so far as those rights extend to the enforcement of another's liability which this Part of this Act prevents that other from excluding or restricting.

Explanatory provisions+N.I.

11 The "reasonableness" test.+N.I.

(1) In relation to a contract term, the requirement of reasonableness for the purposes of this Part of this Act, section 3 of the M6 Misrepresentation Act 1967 and section 3 of the M7 Misrepresentation Act (Northern Ireland) 1967 is that the term shall have been a fair and reasonable one to be included having regard to the circumstances which were, or ought reasonably to have been, known to or in the contemplation of the parties when the contract was made.
(2) In determining for the purposes of section 6 or 7 above whether a contract term satisfies the requirement of reasonableness, regard shall be had in particular to the matters specified in Schedule 2 to this Act; but this subsection does not prevent the court or arbitrator from holding, in accordance with any rule of law, that a term which purports to exclude or restrict any relevant liability is not a term of the contract.
(3) In relation to a notice (not being a notice having contractual effect), the requirement of reasonableness under this Act is that it should be fair and reasonable to allow reliance on it, having regard to all the circumstances obtaining when the liability arose or (but for the notice) would have arisen.
(4) Where by reference to a contract term or notice a person seeks to restrict liability to a specified sum of money, and the question arises (under this or any other Act) whether the term or notice satisfies the requirement of reasonableness, regard shall be had in particular (but without prejudice to subsection (2) above in the case of contract terms) to—
  (a) the resources which he could expect to be available to him for the purpose of meeting the liability should it arise; and
  (b) how far it was open to him to cover himself by insurance.
(5) It is for those claiming that a contract term or notice satisfies the requirement of reasonableness to show that it does.
Marginal Citations
M61967 c. 7
M71967 c. 14. (N.I.)

F19 12 "Dealing as a consumer".+N.I.

. . . .
Amendments (Textual)
F19. S. 12 omitted (1.10.2015 for specified purposes, 1.10.2016 in so far as not already in force) by virtue of Consumer Rights Act 2015 (c. 15), s. 100. (5), Sch. 4 para. 11; S.I. 2015/1630, arts. 3. (g), 4. (c) (with art. 6. (1)(2))

13 Varieties of exemption clause.+N.I.

F20. (1) To the extent that this Part of this Act prevents the exclusion or restriction of any liability it also prevents—
  (a) making the liability or its enforcement subject to restrictive or onerous conditions;
  (b) excluding or restricting any right or remedy in respect of the liability, or subjecting a person to any prejudice in consequence of his pursuing any such right or remedy;
  (c) excluding or restricting rules of evidence or procedure;
and (to that extent) sections 2 [F20, 6 and] 7 also prevent excluding or restricting liability by reference to terms and notices which exclude or restrict the relevant obligation or duty.
(2) But an agreement in writing to submit present or future differences to arbitration is not to be

treated under this Part of this Act as excluding or restricting any liability.
Amendments (Textual)
F20. Words in s. 13. (1) substituted (1.10.2015 for specified purposes, 1.10.2016 in so far as not already in force) by Consumer Rights Act 2015 (c. 15), s. 100. (5), Sch. 4 para. 12; S.I. 2015/1630, arts. 3. (g), 4. (c) (with art. 6. (1)(2))

F21 14 Interpretation of Part I.+N.I.

In this Part of this Act—
"business" includes a profession and the activities of any government department or local or public authority;
[F21"consumer contract" has the same meaning as in the Consumer Rights Act 2015 (see section 61);]
[F21"consumer notice" has the same meaning as in the Consumer Rights Act 2015 (see section 61);]
"goods"has the same meaning as in [F22the Sale of Goods Act 1979];
"hire-purchase agreement" has the same meaning as in the M8 Consumer Credit Act 1974;
"negligence" has the meaning given by section 1. (1);
"notice" includes an announcement, whether or not in writing, and any other communication or pretended communication; and
"personal injury" includes any disease and any impairment of physical or mental condition.
Amendments (Textual)
F21. Words in s. 14 inserted (1.10.2015 for specified purposes, 1.10.2016 in so far as not already in force) by Consumer Rights Act 2015 (c. 15), s. 100. (5), Sch. 4 para. 13; S.I. 2015/1630, arts. 3. (g), 4. (c) (with art. 6. (1)(2))
F22. Words substituted by Sale of Goods Act 1979 (c. 54, SIF 109:1), ss. 62, 63, Sch. 2 para. 20
Marginal Citations
M81974 c. 39

Scope of Part I.

1 Scope of Part I.+N.I.

(1) For the purposes of this Part of this Act, "negligence" means the breach—
  (a) of any obligation, arising from the express or implied terms of a contract, to take reasonable care or exercise reasonable skill in the performance of the contract;
  (b) of any common law duty to take reasonable care or exercise reasonable skill (but not any stricter duty);
  (c) of the common duty of care imposed by the M1 Occupiers' Liability Act 1957 or the M2 Occupiers' Liability Act (Northern Ireland) 1957.
F1. (2)This Part of this Act is subject to Part III; and in relation to contracts, the operation of sections 2 [F1 , 3] and 7 is subject to the exceptions made by Schedule 1.
(3) In the case of both contract and tort, sections 2 to 7 apply (except where the contrary is stated in section 6. (4)) only to business liability, that is liability for breach of obligations or duties arising—
  (a) from things done or to be done by a person in the course of a business (whether his own business or another's); or
  (b) from the occupation of premises used for business purposes of the occupier;
and references to liability are to be read accordingly [F2but liability of an occupier of premises for breach of an obligation or duty towards a person obtaining access to the premises for recreational

or educational purposes, being liability for loss or damage suffered by reason of the dangerous state of the premises, is not a business liability of the occupier unless granting that person such access for the purposes concerned falls within the business purposes of the occupier].

(4) In relation to any breach of duty or obligation, it is, immaterial for any purpose of this Part of this Act whether the breach was inadvertent or intentional, or whether liability for it arises directly or vicariously.

Amendments (Textual)

F1. Words in s. 1. (2) substituted (1.10.2015 for specified purposes, 1.10.2016 in so far as not already in force) by Consumer Rights Act 2015 (c. 15), s. 100. (5), Sch. 4 para. 3; S.I. 2015/1630, arts. 3. (g), 4. (c) (with art. 6. (1)(2))

F2. Words added by Occupiers' Liability Act 1984 (c. 3, SIF 122:2), s. 2 (E.W.) and by the Occupiers' Liability (Northern Ireland) Order 1987 S.I. 1987/1280 (N.I.15), art 4

Marginal Citations

M1 1957 c. 31

M2 1957 c. 25 (N.I.)

Interpretation of Part I.

F1 14 Interpretation of Part I.+N.I.

In this Part of this Act—

"business" includes a profession and the activities of any government department or local or public authority;

[F1"consumer contract" has the same meaning as in the Consumer Rights Act 2015 (see section 61);]

[F1"consumer notice" has the same meaning as in the Consumer Rights Act 2015 (see section 61);]

"goods" has the same meaning as in [F2 the Sale of Goods Act 1979];

"hire-purchase agreement" has the same meaning as in the M1 Consumer Credit Act 1974;

"negligence" has the meaning given by section 1. (1);

"notice" includes an announcement, whether or not in writing, and any other communication or pretended communication; and

"personal injury" includes any disease and any impairment of physical or mental condition.

Amendments (Textual)

F1. Words in s. 14 inserted (1.10.2015 for specified purposes, 1.10.2016 in so far as not already in force) by Consumer Rights Act 2015 (c. 15), s. 100. (5), Sch. 4 para. 13; S.I. 2015/1630, arts. 3. (g), 4. (c) (with art. 6. (1)(2))

F2. Words substituted by Sale of Goods Act 1979 (c. 54, SIF 109:1), ss. 62, 63, Sch. 2 para. 20

Marginal Citations

M1 1974 c. 39

PART II AMENDMENT OF LAW FOR SCOTLAND

PART II S AMENDMENT OF LAW FOR SCOTLAND

15 Scope of Part II.S

(1) This Part of this Act [F1. . .] is subject to Part III of this Act and does not affect the validity, of any discharge or indemnity given by a person in consideration of the receipt by him of compensation in settlement of any claim which he has.

F2. (2)Subject to subsection (3) below, sections 16 [F2and 17] of this Act apply to any contract only to the extent that the contract—

(a) relates to the transfer of the ownership or possession of goods from one person to another (with or without work having been done on them);

(b) constitutes a contract of service or apprenticeship;

(c) relates to services of whatever kind, including (without prejudice to the foregoing generality) carriage, deposit and pledge, care and custody, mandate, agency, loan and services relating to the use of land;

(d) relates to the liability of an occupier of land to persons entering upon or using that land;

(e) relates to a grant of any right or permission to enter upon or use land not amounting to an estate or interest in the land.

F3. (3)Notwithstanding anything in subsection (2) above, sections 16 [F3and 17] —

(a) do not apply to any contract to the extent that the contract—
(i) is a contract of insurance (including a contract to pay annuity on human life);
(ii) relates to the formation, constitution or dissolution of any body corporate or unincorporated association or partnership;

(b) apply to—
a contract of marine salvage or towage;
a charter party of a ship or hovercraft;
a contract for the carriage of goods by ship or hovercraft; or,
a contract to which subsection (4) below relates,
only to the extent that—
(i) both parties deal or hold themselves out as dealing in the course of a business (and then only in so far as the contract purports to exclude or restrict liability for breach of duty in respect of death or personal injury); [F4or]
F4. (ii). . . . .

(4) This subsection relates to a contract in pursuance of which goods are carried by ship or hovercraft and which either—

(a) specifies ship or hovercraft as the means of carriage over part of the journey to be covered; or

(b) makes no provision as to the means of carriage and does not exclude ship or hovercraft as that means,

in so far as the contract operates for and in relation to the carriage of the goods by that means.

Amendments (Textual)

F1. Words in s. 15. (1) repealed (1.4.1991) by Law Reform (Miscellaneous Provisions) (Scotland) Act 1990 (c. 40, SIF 76:2), ss. 68. (2)(6), 74. (2), Sch. 9; S.I. 1991/330, art. 4, Schedule

F2. Words in s. 15. (2) substituted (1.10.2015 for specified purposes, 1.10.2016 in so far as not already in force) by Consumer Rights Act 2015 (c. 15), s. 100. (5), Sch. 4 para. 14. (2); S.I. 2015/1630, arts. 3. (g), 4. (c) (with art. 6. (1)(2))

F3. Words in s. 15. (3) substituted (1.10.2015 for specified purposes, 1.10.2016 in so far as not already in force) by Consumer Rights Act 2015 (c. 15), s. 100. (5), Sch. 4 para. 14. (3)(a); S.I. 2015/1630, arts. 3. (g), 4. (c) (with art. 6. (1)(2))

F4. S. 15. (3)(b)(ii) omitted (1.10.2015 for specified purposes, 1.10.2016 in so far as not already in force) by virtue of Consumer Rights Act 2015 (c. 15), s. 100. (5), Sch. 4 para. 14. (3)(b); S.I. 2015/1630, arts. 3. (g), 4. (c) (with art. 6. (1)(2))

16 Liability for breach of duty.S

(1) [F5. Subject to subsection (1. A) below,] Where a term of a contract [F5, or a provision of a notice given to persons generally or to particular persons,] purports to exclude or restrict liability for breach of duty arising in the course of any business or from the occupation of any premises used for business purposes of the occupier, that term [F5or provision]—
   (a) shall be void in any case where such exclusion or restriction is in respect of death or personal injury;
   (b) shall, in any other case, have no effect if it was not fair and reasonable to incorporate the term in the contract [F5or, as the case may be, if it is not fair and reasonable to allow reliance on the provision].
[F6. (1. A)Nothing in paragraph (b) of subsection (1) above shall be taken as implying that a provision of a notice has effect in circumstances where, apart from that paragraph, it would not have effect.]
(2) Subsection (1)(a) above does not affect the validity of any discharge and indemnity given by a person, on or in connection with an award to him of compensation for pneumoconiosis attributable to employment in the coal industry, in respect of any further claim arising from his contracting that disease.
(3) Where under subsection (1) above a term of a contract [F7or a provision of a notice] is void or has no effect, the fact that a person agreed to, or was aware of, the term [F7or provision] shall not of itself be sufficient evidence that he knowingly and voluntarily assumed any risk.
[F8. (4)This section does not apply to—
   (a) a term in a consumer contract, or
   (b) a notice to the extent that it is a consumer notice,
(but see the provision made about such contracts and notices in sections 62 and 65 of the Consumer Rights Act 2015).]
Amendments (Textual)
F5. Words in s. 16. (1) inserted (1.4.1991) by Law Reform (Miscellaneous Provisions) (Scotland) Act 1990 (c. 40, SIF 76:2), s. 68. (3)(a)(6); S.I. 1991/330, art. 4,Schedule
F6. S. 16. (1. A) inserted (1.4.1991) by Law Reform (Miscellaneous Provisions) (Scotland) Act 1990 (c. 40, SIF 76:2), s. 68. (3)(b)(6); S.I. 1991/330, art. 4,Schedule
F7. Words in s. 16. (3) inserted (1.4.1991) by Law Reform (Miscellaneous Provisions) (Scotland) Act 1990 (c. 40, SIF 76:2), s. 68. (3)(c)(6); S.I. 1991/330, art. 4,Schedule
F8. S. 16. (4) inserted (1.10.2015 for specified purposes, 1.10.2016 in so far as not already in force) by Consumer Rights Act 2015 (c. 15), s. 100. (5), Sch. 4 para. 15; S.I. 2015/1630, arts. 3. (g), 4. (c) (with art. 6. (1)(2))

F917. F9 Control of unreasonable exemptions in ... standard form contracts.S

F10. (1)F10. Any term of a contract which is ... a standard form contract shall have no effect for the purpose of enabling a party to the contract—
   F11. (a)who is in breach of a contractual obligation, to exclude or restrict any liability of his to the F11... customer in respect of the breach;
   F12. (b)in respect of a contractual obligation, to render no performance, or to render a performance substantially different from that which the F12... customer reasonably expected from the contract;
if it was not fair and reasonable to incorporate the term in the contract.
(2) In this section "customer" means a party to a standard form contract who deals on the basis of written standard terms of business of the other party to the contract who himself deals in the course of a business.
[F13. (3)This section does not apply to a term in a consumer contract (but see the provision made about such contracts in section 62 of the Consumer Rights Act 2015).]

Amendments (Textual)
F9. Words in s. 17 omitted (1.10.2015 for specified purposes, 1.10.2016 in so far as not already in force) by virtue of Consumer Rights Act 2015 (c. 15), s. 100. (5), Sch. 4 para. 16. (2); S.I. 2015/1630, arts. 3. (g), 4. (c) (with art. 6. (1)(2))
F10. Words in s. 17. (1) omitted (1.10.2015 for specified purposes, 1.10.2016 in so far as not already in force) by virtue of Consumer Rights Act 2015 (c. 15), s. 100. (5), Sch. 4 para. 16. (3)(a); S.I. 2015/1630, arts. 3. (g), 4. (c) (with art. 6. (1)(2))
F11. Words in s. 17. (1)(a) omitted (1.10.2015 for specified purposes, 1.10.2016 in so far as not already in force) by virtue of Consumer Rights Act 2015 (c. 15), s. 100. (5), Sch. 4 para. 16. (3)(b); S.I. 2015/1630, arts. 3. (g), 4. (c) (with art. 6. (1)(2))
F12. Words in s. 17. (1)(b) omitted (1.10.2015 for specified purposes, 1.10.2016 in so far as not already in force) by virtue of Consumer Rights Act 2015 (c. 15), s. 100. (5), Sch. 4 para. 16. (3)(c); S.I. 2015/1630, arts. 3. (g), 4. (c) (with art. 6. (1)(2))
F13. S. 17. (3) inserted (1.10.2015 for specified purposes, 1.10.2016 in so far as not already in force) by Consumer Rights Act 2015 (c. 15), s. 100. (5), Sch. 4 para. 16. (4); S.I. 2015/1630, arts. 3. (g), 4. (c) (with art. 6. (1)(2))
Modifications etc. (not altering text)
C1. S. 17. (1)(b) extended (1.11.1998 and 1.7.1999 in relation to certain contracts and 7.8.2002 insofar as not then in force) by 1998 c. 20, s. 14. (2) (with s. 12); S.I. 1998/2479, arts. 2, 3; S.I. 1999/1816, art. 3. (1); S.S.I. 2002/337, art. 2

F14 18 Unreasonable indemnity clauses in consumer contracts.S

. . . .
Amendments (Textual)
F14. S. 18 omitted (1.10.2015 for specified purposes, 1.10.2016 in so far as not already in force) by virtue of Consumer Rights Act 2015 (c. 15), s. 100. (5), Sch. 4 para. 17; S.I. 2015/1630, arts. 3. (g), 4. (c) (with art. 6. (1)(2))

F15 19 "Guarantee" of consumer goods.S

. . . .
Amendments (Textual)
F15. S. 19 omitted (1.10.2015) by virtue of Consumer Rights Act 2015 (c. 15), s. 100. (5), Sch. 4 para. 18; S.I. 2015/1630, art. 3. (g) (with art. 6. (1))

20 Obligations implied by law in sale and hire-purchase contracts.S

(1) Any term of a contract which purports to exclude or restrict liability for breach of the obligations arising from—
　(a) section 12 of the Sale of Goods Act [F16 1979] (seller's implied undertakings as to title etc.);
　(b) section 8 of the M1 Supply of Goods (Implied Terms) Act 1973 (implied terms as to title in hire-purchase agreements),
shall be void.
[F17 (1. A) Any term of a contract which purports to exclude or restrict liability for breach of the obligations arising from—
　(a) section 13, 14 or 15 of the 1979 Act (seller's implied undertakings as to conformity of goods with description or sample, or as to their quality or fitness for a particular purpose);
　(b) section 9, 10 or 11 of the 1973 Act (the corresponding things in relation to hire purchase),
shall have effect only if it was fair and reasonable to incorporate the term in the contract.

(1. B)This section does not apply to a consumer contract (but see the provision made about such contracts in section 31 of the Consumer Rights Act 2015).]

F18. (2). . . . .

Amendments (Textual)

F16 "1979" substituted for "1893" by Sale of Goods Act 1979 (c. 54, SIF 109:1), ss. 62, 63, Sch. 2 para. 21

F17. S. 20. (1. A)(1. B) inserted (1.10.2015) by Consumer Rights Act 2015 (c. 15), s. 100. (5), Sch. 4 para. 19. (2); S.I. 2015/1630, art. 3. (g) (with art. 6. (1))

F18. S. 20. (2) omitted (1.10.2015) by virtue of Consumer Rights Act 2015 (c. 15), s. 100. (5), Sch. 4 para. 19. (3); S.I. 2015/1630, art. 3. (g) (with art. 6. (1))

Marginal Citations

M11973 c. 13

21 Obligations implied by law in other contracts for the supply of goods.S

(1) Any term of a contract to which this section applies purporting to exclude or restrict liability for breach of an obligation[F19such as is referred to in subsection (3) below shall have no effect if it was not fair and reasonable to incorporate the term in the contract.]

(2) This section applies to any contract to the extent that it relates to any such matter as is referred to in section 15. (2)(a) of this Act, but does not apply to—

(a) a contract of sale of goods or a hire-purchase agreement; or

(b) a charterparty of a ship or hovercraft F20....

(3) An obligation referred to in this subsection is an obligation incurred under a contract in the course of a business and arising by implication of law from the nature of the contract which relates—

(a) to the correspondence of goods with description or sample, or to the quality or fitness of goods for any particular purpose; or

(b) to any right to transfer ownership or possession of goods, or to the enjoyment of quiet possession of goods.

[F21. (3. A)Notwithstanding anything in the foregoing provisions of this section, any term of a contract which purports to exclude or restrict liability for breach of the obligations arising under section 11. B of the Supply of Goods and Services Act 1982 (implied terms about title, freedom from encumbrances and quiet possession in certain contracts for the transfer of property in goods) shall be void.]

[F22. (3. B)This section does not apply to a consumer contract (but see the provision made about such contracts in section 31 of the Consumer Rights Act 2015).]

(4) F23 . . . .

Amendments (Textual)

F19 Words in s. 21. (1) substituted for s. 21. (1)(a)(b) (1.10.2015) by Consumer Rights Act 2015 (c. 15) , s. 100. (5) , Sch. 4 para. 20. (2) ; S.I. 2015/1630 , art. 3. (g) (with art. 6. (1))

F20 Words in s. 21. (2)(b) omitted (1.10.2015) by virtue of Consumer Rights Act 2015 (c. 15) , s. 100. (5) , Sch. 4 para. 20. (3) ; S.I. 2015/1630 , art. 3. (g) (with art. 6. (1))

F21 S. 21. (3. A) inserted (3.1.1995) by 1982 c. 29 , Pt. I A (as inserted (3.1.1995) by 1994 c. 35 , ss. 6 , 8. (2)(3) , Sch. 1 para.1)

F22 S. 21. (3. B) inserted (1.10.2015) by Consumer Rights Act 2015 (c. 15) , s. 100. (5) , Sch. 4 para. 20. (4) ; S.I. 2015/1630 , art. 3. (g) (with art. 6. (1))

F23 S. 21. (4) repealed (6.4.2005) by The Regulatory Reform (Trading Stamps) Order 2005 (S.I. 2005/871) , art. 6 , Sch.

F2422 Consequence of breach.S

. . . .
Amendments (Textual)
F24. S. 22 omitted (1.10.2015 for specified purposes, 1.10.2016 in so far as not already in force) by virtue of Consumer Rights Act 2015 (c. 15), s. 100. (5), Sch. 4 para. 21; S.I. 2015/1630, arts. 3. (g), 4. (c) (with art. 6. (1)(2))

23 Evasion by means of secondary contract.S

Any term of any contract shall be void which purports to exclude or restrict, or has the effect of excluding or restricting—

  (a) the exercise, by a party to any other contract, of any right or remedy which arises in respect of that other contract in consequence of breach of duty, or of obligation, liability for which could not by virtue of the provisions of this Part of this Act be excluded or restricted by a term of that other contract;

  (b) the application of the provisions of this Part of this Act in respect of that or any other contract.

24 The "reasonableness" test.S

(1) In determining for the purposes of this Part of this Act whether it was fair and reasonable to incorporate a term in a contract, regard shall be had only to the circumstances which were, or ought reasonably to have been, known to or in the contemplation of the parties to the contract at the time the contract was made.

(2) In determining for the purposes of section 20 or 21 of this Act whether it was fair and reasonable to incorporate a term in a contract, regard shall be had in particular to the matters specified in Schedule 2 to this Act; but this subsection shall not prevent a court or arbiter from holding, in accordance with any rule of law, that a term which purports to exclude or restrict any relevant liability is not a term of the contract.

[F25. (2. A)In determining for the purposes of this Part of this Act whether it is fair and reasonable to allow reliance on a provision of a notice (not being a notice having contractual effect), regard shall be had to all the circumstances obtaining when the liability arose or (but for the provision) would have arisen.]

(3) Where a term in a contract [F26or a provision of a notice] purports to restrict liability to a specified sum of money, and the question arises for the purposes of this Part of this Act whether it was fair and reasonable to incorporate the term in the contract [F26or whether it is fair and reasonable to allow reliance on the provision], then, without prejudice to subsection (2) above [F26in the case of a term in a contract], regard shall be had in particular to—

  (a) the resources which the party seeking to rely on that term [F26or provision] could expect to be available to him for the purpose of meeting the liability should it arise;

  (b) how far it was open to that party to cover himself by insurance.

(4) The onus of proving that it was fair and reasonable to incorporate a term in a contract [F27or that it is fair and reasonable to allow reliance on a provision of a notice] shall lie on the party so contending.

Amendments (Textual)
F25. S. 24. (2. A) inserted (1.4.1991) by Law Reform (Miscellaneous Provisions) (Scotland) Act 1990 (c. 40, SIF 76:2), s. 68. (4)(a)(6); S.I. 1991/330, art. 4,Schedule
F26. Words in s. 24. (3) inserted (1.4.1991) by Law Reform (Miscellaneous Provisions) (Scotland) Act 1990 (c. 40, SIF 76:2), s. 68. (4)(b)(6); S.I. 1991/330, art. 4,Schedule
F27. Words in s. 24. (4) inserted (1.4.1991) by Law Reform (Miscellaneous Provisions) (Scotland) Act 1990 (c. 40, SIF 76:2), s. 68. (4)(c)(6); S.I. 1991/330, art. 4,Schedule

25 Interpretation of Part II.S

F28. F29. F30. (1)In this Part of this Act—
"breach of duty" means the breach —
   - of any obligation, arising from the express or implied terms of a contract, to take reasonable care or exercise reasonable skill in the performance of the contract;
   - of any common law duty to take reasonable care or exercise reasonable skill;
   - of the duty of reasonable care imposed by section 2. (1) of the M2 Occupiers' Liability (Scotland) Act 1960;
"business" includes a profession and the activities of any government department or local or public authority;
F30...F30...F30...
[F29"consumer contract" has the same meaning as in the Consumer Rights Act 2015 (see section 61);]
[F28 " consumer notice " has the same meaning as in the Consumer Rights Act 2015 (see section 61);]
"goods" has the same meaning as in [F31the Sale of Goods Act 1979];
"hire-purchase agreement" has the same meaning as in section 189. (1) of the Consumer Credit Act 1974;
[F32 " notice " includes an announcement, whether or not in writing, and any other communication or pretended communication]
"personal injury" includes any disease and any impairment of physical or mental condition.
F33. (1. A)...............................
F33. (1. B)...............................
(2) In relation to any breach of duty or obligation, it is immaterial for any purpose of this Part of this Act whether the act or omission giving rise to that breach was inadvertent or intentional, or whether liability for it arises directly or vicariously.
(3) In this Part of this Act, any reference to excluding or restricting any liability includes—
   (a) making the liability or its enforcement subject to any restrictive or onerous conditions;
   (b) excluding or restricting any right or remedy in respect of the liability, or subjecting a person to any prejudice in consequence of his pursuing any such right or remedy;
   (c) excluding or restricting any rule of evidence or procedure;
   (d) F34
but does not include an agreement to submit any question to arbitration.
(4) F34
F35. (5)In sections 15 [F35, 16, 20 and] 21 of this Act, any reference to excluding or restricting liability for breach of an obligation or duty shall include a reference to excluding or restricting the obligation or duty itself.

Amendments (Textual)
F28. Words in s. 25. (1) inserted (1.10.2015 for specified purposes, 1.10.2016 in so far as not already in force) by Consumer Rights Act 2015 (c. 15), s. 100. (5), Sch. 4 para. 22. (2)(c); S.I. 2015/1630, arts. 3. (g), 4. (c) (with art. 6. (1)(2))
F29. Words in s. 25. (1) substituted (1.10.2015 for specified purposes, 1.10.2016 in so far as not already in force) by Consumer Rights Act 2015 (c. 15), s. 100. (5), Sch. 4 para. 22. (2)(b); S.I. 2015/1630, arts. 3. (g), 4. (c) (with art. 6. (1)(2))
F30. Words in s. 25. (1) omitted (1.10.2015 for specified purposes, 1.10.2016 in so far as not already in force) by virtue of Consumer Rights Act 2015 (c. 15), s. 100. (5), Sch. 4 para. 22. (2)(a); S.I. 2015/1630, arts. 3. (g), 4. (c) (with art. 6. (1)(2))
F31. Words substituted by Sale of Goods Act 1979 (c. 54, SIF 109:1), ss. 62, 63, Sch. 2 para. 22
F32. Definition in s. 25. (1) inserted by Law Reform (Miscellaneous Provisions) (Scotland) Act 1990 (c. 40, SIF 76:2), s. 68. (5)(a)(6); S.I. 1991/330, art. 4, Schedule
F33. S. 25. (1. A)(1. B) omitted (1.10.2015 for specified purposes, 1.10.2016 in so far as not

already in force) by virtue of Consumer Rights Act 2015 (c. 15), s. 100. (5), Sch. 4 para. 22. (3); S.I. 2015/1630, arts. 3. (g), 4. (c) (with art. 6. (1)(2))

F34. S. 25. (3)(d)(4) repealed (1.4.1991) by Law Reform (Miscellaneous Provisions) (Scotland) Act 1990 (c. 40, SIF 76:2), ss. 68. (5)(b)(6); S.I. 1991/330, art. 4,Schedule

F35. Words in s. 25. (5) substituted (1.10.2015 for specified purposes, 1.10.2016 in so far as not already in force) by Consumer Rights Act 2015 (c. 15), s. 100. (5), Sch. 4 para. 22. (4); S.I. 2015/1630, arts. 3. (g), 4. (c) (with art. 6. (1)(2))

Marginal Citations

M21960 c. 30

Scope of Part II.

15 Scope of Part II.S

(1) This Part of this Act [F1. . .] is subject to Part III of this Act and does not affect the validity, of any discharge or indemnity given by a person in consideration of the receipt by him of compensation in settlement of any claim which he has.

F2. (2)Subject to subsection (3) below, sections 16 [F2and 17] of this Act apply to any contract only to the extent that the contract—

(a) relates to the transfer of the ownership or possession of goods from one person to another (with or without work having been done on them);

(b) constitutes a contract of service or apprenticeship;

(c) relates to services of whatever kind, including (without prejudice to the foregoing generality) carriage, deposit and pledge, care and custody, mandate, agency, loan and services relating to the use of land;

(d) relates to the liability of an occupier of land to persons entering upon or using that land;

(e) relates to a grant of any right or permission to enter upon or use land not amounting to an estate or interest in the land.

F3. (3)Notwithstanding anything in subsection (2) above, sections 16 [F3and 17] —

(a) do not apply to any contract to the extent that the contract—

(i) is a contract of insurance (including a contract to pay annuity on human life);

(ii) relates to the formation, constitution or dissolution of any body corporate or unincorporated association or partnership;

(b) apply to—

a contract of marine salvage or towage;

a charter party of a ship or hovercraft;

a contract for the carriage of goods by ship or hovercraft; or,

a contract to which subsection (4) below relates,

only to the extent that—

(i) both parties deal or hold themselves out as dealing in the course of a business (and then only in so far as the contract purports to exclude or restrict liability for breach of duty in respect of death or personal injury); [F4or]

F4. (ii). . . . .

(4) This subsection relates to a contract in pursuance of which goods are carried by ship or hovercraft and which either—

(a) specifies ship or hovercraft as the means of carriage over part of the journey to be covered; or

(b) makes no provision as to the means of carriage and does not exclude ship or hovercraft as that means,

in so far as the contract operates for and in relation to the carriage of the goods by that means.

Amendments (Textual)

F1. Words in s. 15. (1) repealed (1.4.1991) by Law Reform (Miscellaneous Provisions) (Scotland) Act 1990 (c. 40, SIF 76:2), ss. 68. (2)(6), 74. (2), Sch. 9; S.I. 1991/330, art. 4, Schedule

F2. Words in s. 15. (2) substituted (1.10.2015 for specified purposes, 1.10.2016 in so far as not already in force) by Consumer Rights Act 2015 (c. 15), s. 100. (5), Sch. 4 para. 14. (2); S.I. 2015/1630, arts. 3. (g), 4. (c) (with art. 6. (1)(2))

F3. Words in s. 15. (3) substituted (1.10.2015 for specified purposes, 1.10.2016 in so far as not already in force) by Consumer Rights Act 2015 (c. 15), s. 100. (5), Sch. 4 para. 14. (3)(a); S.I. 2015/1630, arts. 3. (g), 4. (c) (with art. 6. (1)(2))

F4. S. 15. (3)(b)(ii) omitted (1.10.2015 for specified purposes, 1.10.2016 in so far as not already in force) by virtue of Consumer Rights Act 2015 (c. 15), s. 100. (5), Sch. 4 para. 14. (3)(b); S.I. 2015/1630, arts. 3. (g), 4. (c) (with art. 6. (1)(2))

Interpretation of Part II.

25 Interpretation of Part II.S

F1. F2. F3. (1)In this Part of this Act—
"breach of duty" means the breach —
 - of any obligation, arising from the express or implied terms of a contract, to take reasonable care or exercise reasonable skill in the performance of the contract;
 - of any common law duty to take reasonable care or exercise reasonable skill;
 - of the duty of reasonable care imposed by section 2. (1) of the M1 Occupiers' Liability (Scotland) Act 1960;
"business" includes a profession and the activities of any government department or local or public authority;
F3...F3...F3...
[F2"consumer contract" has the same meaning as in the Consumer Rights Act 2015 (see section 61);]
[F1 " consumer notice " has the same meaning as in the Consumer Rights Act 2015 (see section 61);]
"goods" has the same meaning as in [F4the Sale of Goods Act 1979];
"hire-purchase agreement" has the same meaning as in section 189. (1) of the Consumer Credit Act 1974;
[F5 " notice " includes an announcement, whether or not in writing, and any other communication or pretended communication]
"personal injury" includes any disease and any impairment of physical or mental condition.
F6. (1. A).............................
F6. (1. B).............................
(2) In relation to any breach of duty or obligation, it is immaterial for any purpose of this Part of this Act whether the act or omission giving rise to that breach was inadvertent or intentional, or whether liability for it arises directly or vicariously.
(3) In this Part of this Act, any reference to excluding or restricting any liability includes—
 (a) making the liability or its enforcement subject to any restrictive or onerous conditions;
 (b) excluding or restricting any right or remedy in respect of the liability, or subjecting a person to any prejudice in consequence of his pursuing any such right or remedy;
 (c) excluding or restricting any rule of evidence or procedure;
 (d)............................. F7
but does not include an agreement to submit any question to arbitration.
(4)............................. F7

F8. (5)In sections 15 [F8, 16, 20 and] 21 of this Act, any reference to excluding or restricting liability for breach of an obligation or duty shall include a reference to excluding or restricting the obligation or duty itself.

Amendments (Textual)

F1. Words in s. 25. (1) inserted (1.10.2015 for specified purposes, 1.10.2016 in so far as not already in force) by Consumer Rights Act 2015 (c. 15), s. 100. (5), Sch. 4 para. 22. (2)(c); S.I. 2015/1630, arts. 3. (g), 4. (c) (with art. 6. (1)(2))

F2. Words in s. 25. (1) substituted (1.10.2015 for specified purposes, 1.10.2016 in so far as not already in force) by Consumer Rights Act 2015 (c. 15), s. 100. (5), Sch. 4 para. 22. (2)(b); S.I. 2015/1630, arts. 3. (g), 4. (c) (with art. 6. (1)(2))

F3. Words in s. 25. (1) omitted (1.10.2015 for specified purposes, 1.10.2016 in so far as not already in force) by virtue of Consumer Rights Act 2015 (c. 15), s. 100. (5), Sch. 4 para. 22. (2)(a); S.I. 2015/1630, arts. 3. (g), 4. (c) (with art. 6. (1)(2))

F4. Words substituted by Sale of Goods Act 1979 (c. 54, SIF 109:1), ss. 62, 63, Sch. 2 para. 22

F5. Definition in s. 25. (1) inserted by Law Reform (Miscellaneous Provisions) (Scotland) Act 1990 (c. 40, SIF 76:2), s. 68. (5)(a)(6); S.I. 1991/330, art. 4, Schedule

F6. S. 25. (1. A)(1. B) omitted (1.10.2015 for specified purposes, 1.10.2016 in so far as not already in force) by virtue of Consumer Rights Act 2015 (c. 15), s. 100. (5), Sch. 4 para. 22. (3); S.I. 2015/1630, arts. 3. (g), 4. (c) (with art. 6. (1)(2))

F7. S. 25. (3)(d)(4) repealed (1.4.1991) by Law Reform (Miscellaneous Provisions) (Scotland) Act 1990 (c. 40, SIF 76:2), ss. 68. (5)(b)(6); S.I. 1991/330, art. 4,Schedule

F8. Words in s. 25. (5) substituted (1.10.2015 for specified purposes, 1.10.2016 in so far as not already in force) by Consumer Rights Act 2015 (c. 15), s. 100. (5), Sch. 4 para. 22. (4); S.I. 2015/1630, arts. 3. (g), 4. (c) (with art. 6. (1)(2))

Marginal Citations

M11960 c. 30

PART III PROVISIONS APPLYING TO WHOLE OF UNITED KINGDOM

PART III PROVISIONS APPLYING TO WHOLE OF UNITED KINGDOM

26 International supply contracts.

(1) The limits imposed by this Act on the extent to which a person may exclude or restrict liability by reference to a contract term do not apply to liability arising under such a contract as is described in subsection (3) below.

F1. (2)The terms of such a contract are not subject to any requirement of reasonableness under section 3 F1...: and nothing in Part 11 of this Act shall require the incorporation of the terms of such a contract to be fair and reasonable for them to have effect.

(3) Subject to subsection (4), that description of contract is one whose characteristics are the following—

(a) either it is a contract of sale of goods or it is one under or in pursuance of which the possession or ownership of goods passes; and

(b) it is made by parties whose places of business (or, if they have none, habitual residences) are in the territories of different States (the Channel Islands and the Isle of Man being treated for this purpose as different States from the United Kingdom).

(4) A contract falls within subsection (3) above only if either—

(a) the goods in question are, at the time of the conclusion of the contract, in the course of carriage, or will be carried, from the territory of one State to the territory of another; or

(b) the acts constituting the offer and acceptance have been done in the territories of different States; or

(c) the contract provides for the goods to be delivered to the territory of a State other than that within whose territory those acts were done.

Amendments (Textual)

F1. Words in s. 26. (2) omitted (1.10.2015 for specified purposes, 1.10.2016 in so far as not already in force) by virtue of Consumer Rights Act 2015 (c. 15), s. 100. (5), Sch. 4 para. 23; S.I. 2015/1630, arts. 3. (g), 4. (c) (with art. 6. (1)(2))

27 Choice of law clauses.

(1) Where the [F2law applicable to] a contract is the law of any part of the United Kingdom only by choice of the parties (and apart from that choice would be the law of some country outside the United Kingdom) sections 2 to 7 and 16 to 21 of this Act do not operate as part [F2of the law applicable to the contract].

F3. (2)F3. This Act has effect notwithstanding any contract term which applies or purports to apply the law of some country outside the United Kingdom, where ...—

(a) the term appears to the court, or arbitrator or arbiter to have been imposed wholly or mainly for the purpose of enabling the party imposing it to evade the operation of this Act; F4...

F4. (b)...............................

F5. (3)...............................

Amendments (Textual)

F2. Words in s. 27. (1) substituted (1.4.1991) by Contracts (Applicable Law) Act 1990 (c. 36, SIF 30), s. 5, Sch. 4 para. 4; S.I. 1991/707, art. 2

F3. Words in s. 27. (2) omitted (1.10.2015 for specified purposes, 1.10.2016 in so far as not already in force) by virtue of Consumer Rights Act 2015 (c. 15), s. 100. (5), Sch. 4 para. 24. (2)(a); S.I. 2015/1630, arts. 3. (g), 4. (c) (with art. 6. (1)(2))

F4. S. 27. (2)(b) omitted (1.10.2015 for specified purposes, 1.10.2016 in so far as not already in force) by virtue of Consumer Rights Act 2015 (c. 15), s. 100. (5), Sch. 4 para. 24. (2)(b); S.I. 2015/1630, arts. 3. (g), 4. (c) (with art. 6. (1)(2))

F5. S. 27. (3) omitted (1.10.2015 for specified purposes, 1.10.2016 in so far as not already in force) by virtue of Consumer Rights Act 2015 (c. 15), s. 100. (5), Sch. 4 para. 24. (3); S.I. 2015/1630, arts. 3. (g), 4. (c) (with art. 6. (1)(2))

F628 Temporary provision for sea carriage passengers.

....

Amendments (Textual)

F6. S. 28 omitted (1.10.2015 for specified purposes, 1.10.2016 in so far as not already in force) by virtue of Consumer Rights Act 2015 (c. 15), s. 100. (5), Sch. 4 para. 25; S.I. 2015/1630, arts. 3. (g), 4. (c) (with art. 6. (1)(2))

29 Saving for other relevant legislation.

(1) Nothing in this Act removes or restricts the effect of, or prevents reliance upon, any contractual provision which—

(a) is authorised or required by the express terms or necessary implication of an enactment; or

(b) being made with a view to compliance with an international agreement to which the United

Kingdom is a party, does not operate more restrictively than is contemplated by the agreement.
(2) A contract term is to be taken—
  (a) for the purposes of Part I of this Act, as satisfying the requirement of reasonableness; and
  (b) for those of Part 11, to have been fair and reasonable to incorporate,
if it is incorporated or approved by, or incorporated pursuant to a decision or ruling of, a competent authority acting in the exercise of any statutory jurisdiction or function and is not a term in a contract to which the competent authority is itself a party.
(3) In this section—
"competent authority" means any court, arbitrator or arbiter, government department or public authority;
"enactment" means any legislation (including subordinate legislation) of the United Kingdom or Northern Ireland and any instrument having effect by virtue of such legislation; and
"statutory" means conferred by an enactment.
Modifications etc. (not altering text)
C1. S. 29. (1) modified by Telecommunications Act 1984 (c. 12, SIF 96), s. 109, Sch. 5 para. 12. (7)

30. . . . . F7.

Amendments (Textual)
F7. S. 30 repealed by Consumer Safety Act 1978 (c. 38), s. 10. (1), Sch. 3

General

31 Commencement; amendments; repeals.

(1) This Act comes into force on 1st February 1978.
(2) Nothing in this Act applies to contracts made before the date on which it comes into force; but subject to this, it applies to liability for any loss or damage which is suffered on or after that date.
X1. (3) The enactments specified in Schedule 3 to this Act are amended as there shown.
X1. (4) The enactments specified in Schedule 4 to this Act are repealed to the extent specified in column 3 of that Schedule.
Editorial Information
X1. The text of s. 31. (3)(4) is in the form in which it was originally enacted: it was not reproduced in Statutes in Force and does not reflect any amendments or repeals which may have been made prior to 1.2.1991.

32 Citation and extent.

(1) This Act may be cited as the Unfair Contract Terms Act 1977.
(2) Part I of this Act extends to England and Wales and to Northern Ireland; but it does not extend to Scotland.
(3) Part II of this Act extends to Scotland only.
(4) This Part of this Act extends to the whole of the United Kingdom.

Schedules

Schedule 1. Scope of Sections 2, 3 and 7

Section 1. (2).
Amendments (Textual)
F1. Words in Sch. 1 substituted (1.10.2015 for specified purposes, 1.10.2016 in so far as not already in force) by Consumer Rights Act 2015 (c. 15), s. 100. (5), Sch. 4 para. 26. (2); S.I. 2015/1630, arts. 3. (g), 4. (c) (with art. 6. (1)(2))
F2. F11. Sections 2 [F2and 3] of this Act do not extend to—+N.I.
(a) any contract of insurance (including a contract to pay an annuity on human life);
(b) any contract so far as it relates to the creation or transfer of an interest in land, or to the termination of such an interest, whether by extinction, merger, surrender, forfeiture or otherwise;
(c) any contract so far as it relates to the creation or transfer of a right or interest in any patent, trade mark, copyright [F3or design right], registered design, technical or commercial information or other intellectual property, or relates to the termination of any such right or interest;
(d) any contract so far as it relates—
(i) to the formation or dissolution of a company (which means any body corporate or unincorporated association and includes a partnership), or
(ii) to its constitution or the rights or obligations of its corporators or members;
(e) any contract so far as it relates to the creation or transfer of securities or of any right or interest in securities.
[F4. (f) anything that is governed by Article 6 of Regulation (EU) No 181/2011 of the European Parliament and of the Council of 16 February 2011 concerning the rights of passengers in bus and coach transport and amending Regulation (EC) No 2006/2004 .]
Amendments (Textual)
F2. Words in Sch. 1 para. 1 substituted (1.10.2015 for specified purposes, 1.10.2016 in so far as not already in force) by Consumer Rights Act 2015 (c. 15), s. 100. (5), Sch. 4 para. 26. (3); S.I. 2015/1630, arts. 3. (g), 4. (c) (with art. 6. (1)(2))
F3. Words inserted by Copyright, Designs and Patents Act 1988 (c. 48, SIF 67. A), s. 303. (1), Sch. 7 para. 24
F4. Sch. 1 para. 1. (f) inserted (E.W.S.) (19.8.2013) by The Rights of Passengers in Bus and Coach Transport (Exemptions and Enforcement) Regulations 2013 (S.I. 2013/1865), regs. 1. (1), 13. (5)
Modifications etc. (not altering text)
C1. Sch. 1 para. 1. (c) extended by Patents, Designs and Marks Act 1986 (c. 39, SIF 67. A), ss. 2. (3), 4. (7), Sch. para. 1. (2)(f)
C2. Sch. 1 para. 1. (c) extended by S.I. 1987/1497, reg. 9. (2), sch. 2. Sch. 1 para. 1. (c) amended (31.10.1994) by 1994 c. 26, s. 106. (1), Sch. 4 para. 1. (1)(2); S.I. 1994/2550, art.2
F5. F1. F62. Section 2. (1) extends to—+N.I.
(a) any contract of marine salvage or towage;
(b) any charterparty of a ship or hovercraft; and
(c) any contract for the carriage of goods by ship or hovercraft;
but subject to this sections 2 [F5 , 3] and 7 do not extend to any such contract F6....
Amendments (Textual)
F1. Words in Sch. 1 substituted (1.10.2015 for specified purposes, 1.10.2016 in so far as not already in force) by Consumer Rights Act 2015 (c. 15), s. 100. (5), Sch. 4 para. 26. (2); S.I. 2015/1630, arts. 3. (g), 4. (c) (with art. 6. (1)(2))
F5. Word in Sch. 1 para. 2 substituted (1.10.2015 for specified purposes, 1.10.2016 in so far as not already in force) by Consumer Rights Act 2015 (c. 15), s. 100. (5), Sch. 4 para. 26. (4)(a); S.I. 2015/1630, arts. 3. (g), 4. (c) (with art. 6. (1)(2))
F6. Words in Sch. 1 para. 2 omitted (1.10.2015 for specified purposes, 1.10.2016 in so far as not already in force) by virtue of Consumer Rights Act 2015 (c. 15), s. 100. (5), Sch. 4 para. 26. (4)(b); S.I. 2015/1630, arts. 3. (g), 4. (c) (with art. 6. (1)(2))

F7. F8. F13. Where goods are carried by ship or hovercraft in pursuance of a contract which either—+N.I.
(a) specifies that as the means of carriage over part of the journey to be covered, or
(b) makes no provision as to the means of carriage and does not exclude that means,
then sections 2. (2)[F7and 3] do notF8... extend to the contract as it operates for and in relation to the carriage of the goods by that means.
Amendments (Textual)
F1. Words in Sch. 1 substituted (1.10.2015 for specified purposes, 1.10.2016 in so far as not already in force) by Consumer Rights Act 2015 (c. 15), s. 100. (5), Sch. 4 para. 26. (2); S.I. 2015/1630, arts. 3. (g), 4. (c) (with art. 6. (1)(2))
F7. Words in Sch. 1 para. 3 substituted (1.10.2015 for specified purposes, 1.10.2016 in so far as not already in force) by Consumer Rights Act 2015 (c. 15), s. 100. (5), Sch. 4 para. 26. (5)(a); S.I. 2015/1630, arts. 3. (g), 4. (c) (with art. 6. (1)(2))
F8. Words in Sch. 1 para. 3 omitted (1.10.2015 for specified purposes, 1.10.2016 in so far as not already in force) by virtue of Consumer Rights Act 2015 (c. 15), s. 100. (5), Sch. 4 para. 26. (5)(b); S.I. 2015/1630, arts. 3. (g), 4. (c) (with art. 6. (1)(2))
4. Section 2. (1) and (2) do not extend to a contract of employment, except in favour of the employee.+N.I.
5. Section 2. (1) does not affect the validity of any discharge and indemnity given by a person, on or in connection with an award to him of compensation for pneumoconiosis attributable to employment in the coal industry, in respect of any further claim arising from his contracting that disease.+N.I.

Schedule 2. "Guidelines" for Application of Reasonableness Test

Sections 11. (2) and 24. (2).
Amendments (Textual)
F1. Words in Sch. 2 substituted (1.10.2015 for specified purposes, 1.10.2016 in so far as not already in force) by Consumer Rights Act 2015 (c. 15), s. 100. (5), Sch. 4 para. 27; S.I. 2015/1630, arts. 3. (g), 4. (c) (with art. 6. (1)(2))

The matters to which regard is to be had in particular for the purposes of sections [F16. (1. A), 7. (1. A) and (4),] 20 and 21 are any of the following which appear to be relevant—
(a) the strength of the bargaining positions of the parties relative to each other, taking into account (among other things) alternative means by which the customer's requirements could have been met;
(b) whether the customer received an inducement to agree to the term, or in accepting it had an opportunity of entering into a similar contract with other persons, but without having a similar term;
(c) whether the customer knew or ought reasonably to have known of the existence and the extent of the term (having regard, among other things, to any custom of the trade and any previous course of dealing between the parties);
(d) where the term excludes or restricts any relevant liability if some condition was not complied with, whether it was reasonable at the time of the contract to expect that compliance with that condition would be practicable;
(e) whether the goods were manufactured, processed or adapted to the special order of the customer.

Schedule 3. Amendments of Enactments

Section 31. (3).
Editorial Information
X1. The text of Sch. 3 is in the form in which it was originally enacted: it was not reproduced in Statutes in Force and does not reflect any amendments or repeals which may have been made prior to 1.2.1991.

. . . . F1
Amendments (Textual)
F1. Entries repealed by Sale of goods Act 1979 (c. 54, SIF 109:1), s. 62, Sch. 3

In the M1 Supply of Goods (Implied Terms) Act 1973 as originally enacted and as substituted by the M2 Consumer Credit Act 1974)—
(a) in section 14. (1) for the words from "conditional sale" to the end substitute " a conditional sale agreement where the buyer deals as a consumer within Part I of the Unfair Contract Terms Act 1977. . . . . F2 ";
(b) in section 15. (1), in the definition of " business", for "local authority or statutory undertaker" substitute " or local or public authority ".
Amendments (Textual)
F2. Words repealed by Statute Law (Repeals) Act 1981 (c. 19), Sch. Pt. XII
Marginal Citations
M11973 c. 13
M21974 c. 39

Schedule 4. Repeals

Section 31. (4).
Editorial Information
X1. The text of Sch. 4 is in the form in which it was originally enacted: it was not reproduced in Statutes in Force and does not reflect any amendments or repeals which may have been made prior to 1.2.1991.

Chapter	Short title	Extent of repeal
56&57 Vict. c. 71.	Sale of Goods Act 1893.	In section 55, subsections (3) to (11).
		Section 55A.
		Section 61(6).
		In section 62(1) the definition of "contract for the international sale of goods".
1962 c. 46.	Transport Act 1962.	Section 43(7).
1967 c. 45	Uniform Laws on International Sales Act 1967.	In section 1(4), the words "55and 55A".
1972 c. 33.	Carriage by Railway Act 1972.	In section 1(1), the words from "contract for the international sale of goods" onwards.
1973 c. 13.	Supply of Goods (Implied Terms) Act 1973.	Section 5(1).
		Section 6.

	In section 7(1), the words from "contract for the international sale of goods" onwards.
	In section 12, subsections (2) to (9).
	Section 13.
	In section 15(1), the definition of "consumer sale".

The repeals in sections 12 and 15 of the Supply of Goods (Implied Terms) Act 1973 shall have effect in relation to those sections as originally enacted and as substituted by the M1 Consumer Credit Act 1974.
Marginal Citations
M11974 c. 39

Open Government Licence v3.0

Contains public sector information licensed under the Open Government Licence v3.0.
The full licence if available at the following address:
http://www.nationalarchives.gov.uk/doc/open-government-licence/version/3/

Printed in Great Britain
by Amazon